How to Get on the News without Committing Murder

How to Get on the News without Committing Murder

8 Killer Tips for a Positive Media Image at Midlife

Beverly Mahone

Benoham Publishing

A Division of BAMedia

How to Get on the News without Committing Murder

8 Killer Tips for a Positive Media Image

First Printing, February 2012

Published by

Benoham Publishing
P.O. Box 11037
Durham, NC 27703

www.beverlymahone.com

Sandra Holcombe, SDH Productions
Copy Editor

sdhproductions@juno.com

Ginger Marks, DocUmeant Designs
Book layout & Cover design

www.DocuMeantDesigns.com

Printed in the United States of America
Distributed by DocUmeant Publishing

ISBN-13 9780977887613
ISBN-10 0-977-8876-1-8

RAVES

"How to Get on the News without Committing Murder is the handiest, most useful guide I've seen since social media came about. It's all here."

Judy Schriener, *journalist, author, radio show host*

"This book is all substance and no fluff. If you are looking to create a presence for yourself in the media, Bev Mahone's expertise will prove invaluable."

Dave Baldwin, *writer and editor*

"As a former TV anchor and an accredited PR professional, How to Get On the News Without Committing Murder, gives readers smart tips to

increase their visibility and credibility by working with the media THE RIGHT WAY. Beverly shares great ideas to show you how to take advantage of the assets you already have so you can step into the spotlight with ease and grace."

Shannon Cherry, APR, MA, *Amazon bestselling author, professional speaker and PR expert*

"Beverly Mahone hits the public relations nail right on the head for us boomerpreneurs! Bev is a pro in her field. Any boomerpreneur ready to break out, take the world by storm and make her mark, would do herself a big favor to review and implement Beverly's experienced, and expert, advice."

Linda Alexander, *Author/Social Archeologist*
http://www.lindajalexander.net

CONTENTS

FOREWORD

I first met Beverly Mahone in 2004 on what was then an up-and-coming new social networking site for business people called Ryze. Unfortunately, the site was not able to keep up with the technological changes taking place in the world and we lost touch for a while.

Then in 2008, we reconnected on Twitter and Facebook®. While I feel I have stagnated, to a degree, I have noticed great movement from her.

Beverly started her social media quest with an online radio program, graduated to a regular radio show, and then to a television show, all in the space of three years.

I have been on two of her radio programs; I don't live close enough to be on her TV show. What has impressed me more than anything else is her ability to not only help others get publicity and exposure, but how she's been able to attract people you wouldn't think a local personality could get. For instance, she's had both Jane Velez-Mitchell and Bern Nadette Stanis on her program, as well as, a host of other celebrities. She has also talked with some big-time Internet stars and invited some of them onto her programs.

If there is anyone who has proven they not only talk-the-talk but walk-the-walk when it comes to getting known by the news media, or media in general, it's Beverly. I have seen the videos of her on local TV news and those local news programs that cover community issues.

She's a former newsperson herself, so she knows her way around.

Frankly, she's had to give me advice on publicizing myself. Ideas I would not have thought of on my own, because like most people, I was taught that it's not nice to brag about yourself.

It's not about bragging, though; *it's about publicity.* It's about making sure other people know who you are and what you do and how they may use what you have to offer. It's about leveraging tactics for everyone's benefit, including yours. It's about shared interests, because when promoting yourself, you help to promote others as well. It's about accessing all the things that are out there to help give you a voice for the masses. Beverly's great at teaching us these things; anyone can learn from her lessons and approach—and that's why you need this book.

If you want to stand out, want to connect with the media, want to be a media darling, want to be seen as an expert . . . if you want to be the first person that local or even national media calls for a sound bite on something your business represents, this is the book for you.

If I can paraphrase something she says in this book, if people aren't beating down your door or blowing up your email and telephone trying to reach you, then you need to find them and take action.

Through the lessons you will garner in this book, Bev will help you do that very thing. Look how her lessons have worked for me; I've written a Foreword in a book; and . . . I didn't have to murder anyone!

T. T. "Mitch" Mitchell
T. T. Mitchell Consulting, Inc.
www.ttmitchellconsulting.com

ACKNOWLEDGEMENTS

I am grateful to every news director who hired me and allowed me to prove my qualifications and skills.

I am honored and privileged to have spent three decades in the broadcast industry.

I am thankful that my parents' money didn't go to waste at Ohio University. I learned how to become a real journalist with the help of Dr. Dru Evarts, Don Lambert, Eric Moore, WOUB Radio and The Post campus newspaper.

My appreciation goes out to best-selling author Linda Alexander, Joan Stewart better known as The Publicity Hound®, fellow journalist, author and radio show host Judy Schriener, PR expert, Shannon Cherry, writer Dave Baldwin and

SEO expert Mitch Mitchell for their reviews of this book.

Gratitude and love to Ginger Marks, my awesome graphics designer who always sees my vision as I do and to Sandra Holcombe, who can clean up my grammatical errors while keeping my voice intact. That takes a special skill.

Every woman needs a friend she can call on when needing help with personal branding and image. I'm blessed to have Personal Brand Strategist Cynthia White as that "you can call me anytime" friend.

They say the camera doesn't lie but a good photographer can make you look really fabulous. Thank you Evan L. Grant of by: Grant Photography.

If it weren't for Heidi Caswell, I would still be driving my husband crazy with trying to help me navigate my website. Heidi is a WordPress Pro and because of her teaching, I have learned how to create my own unique presence on the Internet.

Finally, I am thankful for my husband Nate, who continues to be the wind beneath my wings.

INTRODUCTION

BREAKING NEWS… This Just In:

*"Police are on the lookout for **(Insert your name here)**, a middle-aged corporate-America employee wanted for questioning in connection with the murder of a younger colleague. The victim's body was found in the employee conference room, where it was initially believed he was taking a nap.*

Meanwhile, police say they've received statements from sources close to the victim indicating (insert your last name only) was jealous of the fact that the victim was becoming a mega star in the company they worked for, even though he was 15 years *younger. If you see THIS PERSON **(your***

picture now posted on the television

***screen),** use extreme caution for he/she*

may be armed and dangerous. You are

asked to notify police immediately!"

◦ ◦ ◦ ◦ ◦ ○○○○○○○○○○○○○○○○○ ◦ ◦ ◦ ◦

During my years as a radio and television news reporter, producer and assignment editor, the unwritten rule during editorial meetings was: "If it bleeds it leads"—the more *gruesome* the better. Surely, you would never consider going to such extremes in an effort to get media exposure, but you can certainly have your time to shine in the media spotlight.

As a veteran journalist with more than 30 years of experience, I invite you to use this book as a guide to help you promote who you are and what you do—so the media will take an interest *and* want to feature you on the news, a talk show or in a newspaper article.

I'm providing eight killer steps to help you in presenting a positive media image. What you choose to do with them is on you, but the fact that you purchased this book says you're moving in the right direction.

Killer Tip #1

USE YOUR AGE

AND EXPERIENCE

AS ADVANTAGES

"Aging is not 'lost youth' but a new stage of opportunity and strength." —*Bernard Baruch*

Don't let age hold you back when looking for your time to shine in the media spotlight. Age is truly irrelevant. When seeking media attention, you have more important things to worry about than age. You should be focused on making sure you have a compelling message.

TV, radio, and newspapers receive hundreds of press releases every day, so how do journalists choose the ones to feature? They decide by selecting the ones that come across as being the most interesting to their readers, listeners, or viewers.

You can actually use age to your advantage. Being a "mature" expert in your field can help you shine above the rest. Being able to offer comparisons on subjects or products years ago versus now can open up an interesting dialogue between you and that young journalist who will probably interview you.

Age is only a factor if you make it one—by being a know-it-all, difficult to communicate with, and trying to tell the journalist how to do his or her job. You certainly don't want to be known by media types as a crotchety old fuddy-duddy.

The media doesn't care how old you are when it comes to who they choose to interview. As a matter of fact, your age, wisdom, and experience could work to your advantage when it comes to certain stories.

BUT . . .

Your age can work to your disadvantage if you let it. What does that mean? It means no young journalist is impressed by an "I-know-it-all 50-something," so here are some tips on how you can interview well without coming across as an old jerk:

(1) *Don't make the reporter feel dumb:* Some young reporters may already be intimidated by your knowledge, age, and experience, so don't make them feel stupid by saying, "I know you wouldn't know anything about that" or "That

was before your time."
They already know that.

(2) *Don't be a smart-aleck:*
Don't come across as if
you're doing the reporter a
favor by giving them an
interview because, in reality,
you aren't. They can always
find someone else.

(3) *Don't complain:* Don't get
upset because you said
much more than they were
able to put on the air. Or
perhaps they decided not to
use your interview at all.
Calling and complaining
about your lack of face time
won't accomplish anything.
And trust me, your name
will be scratched off that
reporter's list for any
follow-up interviews.

(4) *Don't take over:* It's NOT
your show. Allow the

reporter to guide you with questions. In the end, most will ask if you have anything else you want to add. That's your cue to offer more relevant information to the subject matter—but don't keep rambling for the next 15 to 20 minutes, because it will surely get edited (if it's a pre-recorded interview).

(5) *Be gracious:* Reporters always appreciate a thank-you note with a message letting them know how grateful you are they contacted you ... and that you're willing to talk to them again if they need you.

Make it your time to shine in the media spotlight, and let your age work for you and not against you.

Now, let's start creating a buzz ...

Killer Tip #2

CREATE A

BUZZ!

"Publicity can be terrible. But only if you don't have any."   *—Actress Jane Russell*

Silence may be golden to the parents of a rambunctious child, but according to actor Samuel L. Jackson, "If you have an opportunity to use your voice you should use it." Here's the deal: No one's ever going to know anything about you unless you tell them. As a small-business owner or "boomerpreneur," you can't sit back and rest on the laurels of your Employee of the Year award from

1985. The media doesn't care about your resume. You have to learn how to transfer your work history from corporate America by taking the best of your resume and turning it into your expertise. Once you've done that, you have to get up, make some noise, and create a "media buzz." You have to market yourself in such a way that draws media attention to you and provides visibility.

Getting media exposure is a competitive process. You have to keep in mind there are literally thousands of other people who are doing the same thing or something similar to what you're doing and, just like you, they think they're the absolute best at it.

On top of that, they may be younger, more tech savvy and better looking—but what can set you apart from them is your ability to get your name out there to make journalists take notice.

Communication is the key to effective marketing and one of the best ways to communicate via social media is through blogging. Blogging is a great way for baby boomers to demonstrate their expertise, exchange ideas and generate some free publicity.

The one advantage we, as baby boomers, have over the younger generation is the ability to communicate face to face. We grew up in an era when we talked to each other instead of through a computer or text messaging. So take your effective communication skills and start tooting your own horn.

Okay, I can hear you now:

> "I feel uncomfortable talking about myself."

"I don't want to come across as sounding obnoxious."

"It's hard for me to talk about myself because I'm not sure what to say."

"I am not a self-absorbed person, so I don't feel the need to promote myself."

"I think of tooting my own horn as bragging."

Now let me say here that there is a difference between letting others know about your accomplishments and simply bragging about how good you are. For example, which press release headline would turn you off?

Barbara Jones Credits Her Skills as Reason for Winning Best Virtual Assistant Award in North Carolina

OR ...

Barbara Jones Awarded Highest Virtual Assistant Honor for North Carolina

Get the point?

Here are my tips on how to make some noise with the press:

Start a blog. Blogs have become another resource for journalists in their quest to look for interesting news stories and people to interview. If you have a particular subject you are passionate about write about it and keep writing. You can also use your blog as a platform to discuss a variety of issues but make sure it sticks to a similar theme. For example, if you're writing about beauty and aging, you could cover a wide variety of sub-topics that not only deals with the physical aspects—but also covers the emotional side of it.

Be consistent with your blog. You don't have to write everyday, but try to write a minimum of two times a week and make sure you post your blog(s) in places where they can be found. Pingomatic, Technorati™, Digg, Feedburner, Google and Yahoo are just a few of the sites journalists check. If you're on Facebook you can submit it to NetworkedBlogs. (see resource page).

In a national survey conducted by Cision and Don Bates of George Washington University in 2009[1], it was learned that an overwhelming majority of reporters and editors depend on social media sources when researching their stories. Among the journalists surveyed, eighty-nine percent said they turn to blogs for story research, sixty-five

---

[1] George Washington University and Cision.com, *2009 Social Media & Online Usage Study* , 2009 December, http://www.gwu.edu/~newsctr/10/pdfs/gw_cision_sm_study_09.PDF

percent to social media sites such as Facebook and LinkedIn, and fifty-two percent to microblogging services like Twitter.

If you don't see blogging in your immediate future, perhaps you can take advantage of any outstanding achievements or awards you receive. That's always worth a mention in the press, especially if you can tie it into some other relevant news. For example: Let's say you've been named Outstanding Insurance Salesperson of the Month. You can take the opportunity to create a news angle by offering tips on how people can save money when purchasing insurance or what type of insurance scams the elderly should avoid.

Another way to create a buzz about yourself is by leading people to the positive things that are being written about you. This could be in the form of a blog post, a quote in an article or a testimonial about the great work you do.

I was featured in a *New York Times* article a few years back because a reporter saw some of my articles on a site called Authors Den (see resource page). Once the article was published, complete with a nice-sized color photo of me on the front page, I sent the link to everyone I knew—and even strangers who just happened to be on my email mailing list—because I wanted them to see what had been written about me. The fact that the *Times* had written about me boosted my credibility—not only as an author but also as a babyboomer expert, and it also got me additional media interviews and increased my book sales.

You can also get a lot of mileage out of promoting others. Actually, one of the best ways to promote yourself is by promoting someone else.

What does that mean? Perhaps you see someone on Twitter, Facebook, LinkedIn™, MySpace®, etc., you think is very good at what they do. You can use your blog to write about them—or if you have a radio show, you can invite them to come on as a guest and then promote that you're interviewing them. You could also write an article using their expert opinion or advice about the subject matter you're writing about.

By promoting others, you are not only creating attention about the other person, but you are also drawing attention to yourself. It's a win-win situation because you're guaranteed to have the person you're promoting talk about you in return. As a result, you can develop an entirely new following, and those new followers will begin to learn more about you and what you do. If you promote others well, a follower could turn into a new client or customer.

Now let's work on building those media relationships.

Killer Tip #3

BUILD MEDIA

RELATIONSHIPS

"The quality of your life is the quality of your relationships." —Anthony Robbins, Author, Speaker and Motivational Guru

Local radio and television news isn't what it used to be. There was a time when stations focused primarily and very seriously on their news content. Today, however, some could argue that many news programs have become an entertainment showcase with model-type-looking anchors and news content that's either sensationalized or inaccurate.

Nevertheless, you can still seize the opportunity to build relationships with journalists.

Cultivate relationships with the media. Determine which media outlets are a good fit for you and work to build relationships with them. For example, if you're in the business of selling hearing aids or life insurance, you might not generate much of a listening audience on a hip-hop station.

Some radio and television stations cater to an older audience so do your homework and find out about their major demographic. You can do this by researching on Arbitron.com or simply calling the station's sales department and asking them to share that information with you.

Warning: If you call, don't let a salesperson try to hoodwink you into purchasing airtime.

Build a contact list. If you just happen to be in a location where news is happening and you see a reporter, be a "Mrs. Kravitz." You remember her. She was that nosey neighbor on *Bewitched* who never hesitated to find out what was going on around her. You shouldn't hesitate either. Walk over and find out what's going on. Then introduce yourself, exchange business cards, and briefly let them know what you do. Who knows? You may have an expertise that connects to their story, or they may just want to interview you for your perspective.

But, beware of one thing: reporters hate having someone interrupt them for long periods of time when they're out covering a story, because they're on a deadline. Say what you have to say, and let them know you'll contact them later. Then make sure you do it—like the next day.

Another suggestion: Don't be picky about which station you'd like to appear on. Your favorite news may be on the local NBC station, but when you look for publicity, be ready to receive it from the first station that contacts you. Also, journalists love "exclusives," so if you have an incredible story to tell, let the producer know you'll give it to their station only.

Another way to establish and build a media-contact list is to single out specific journalists and write them a letter. Let them know you're available for interviews whenever they do a story on your topic. Include your business card and be sure to list all contact information. If you have a book you've written or a published article, send it along for added credibility.

I should add that some journalists like to have their egos stroked, so it certainly wouldn't hurt to let them know how much you enjoy watching or listening to them on the news. You might even choose to make references to a particular story you saw them cover.

Knowing who's who in the media will help you complete your list. Never send information to "Editor" and assume it will reach the right person. Names of reporters are easy to get because you see them daily and you can find them on the station's website, but the real decision makers are generally behind the scenes. You can find out who they are by simply picking up your phone and calling the newsroom. As a matter of fact, I recommend you contact the media outlet to find out how they prefer to receive information. Don't assume everyone wants to read your news in an email.

Here are some of the key people to know in radio and television:

- **News Director** – Leads the newsroom and determines what news goes on the air.

- **Assignment Editor** – Handles all news releases.

- **Producers** – Responsible for creating the newscast. They, along with the news director, decide what stories will air in the different newscasts (or talk show).

- **Community Service Director** – Contact for public service announcements (PSAs), talk shows, or community-calendar listings.

- **Web Content Producer** – This person creates video content made specifically for distribution on the Internet from a station's website.

Don't rule anyone out. Do your homework and find those journalists you'd like to establish contact with. This includes newspaper reporters (on and offline), Internet radio hosts, and podcasters. The broader your contact list is, the more opportunities you will have for exposure.

When you've established contact, make sure you work on developing a rapport, but don't be pushy. Once the media sees you as someone they like and trust, you'll be on your way to shining in the media spotlight.

Now let me show you how to shine with that all-important press release.

Killer Tip #4

LEARN HOW TO

WRITE A DYNAMIC

PRESS RELEASE

"Regardless of the changes in technology, the market for well-crafted messages will always have an audience."   —*Steve Burnett,*
                                  The Burnett Group

Newsroom editors receive tons of press releases daily. What you may be surprised to learn is more than half of those releases are tossed. Some of them are never even read. When I worked on the assignment desk, I probably deleted two-thirds of the press releases that were sent by email. Why? Many times the release was poorly written. Sometimes people used the release to sell their products, and then there were those releases that said nothing at all.

As boomers we grew up during the years when knowing how to spell the whole word was important, and writing a complete sentence and paragraph was a prerequisite for just about everything—so we do have an advantage.

Here are a few tips to help you as you prepare to write a good press release:

Is your news "newsworthy"? The purpose of a press release is to inform the world of your news item. Do not use your press release to try and make a sale. A good press release answers all of the "W" questions (who, what, where, when, and why), providing the media with useful information about your organization, product, service, or event. If your press release reads like you're trying to sell something, you need to rewrite it.

Start strong. Your headline and first paragraph should tell the story. The rest of your press release should provide the details. You have a few seconds to grab the attention of your readers. If the headline and first sentence don't entice them, chances are the rest of the release won't be read.

Write for the Media. On occasion, media outlets, especially online media, will pick up your press release and run it in their publications with little or no modification. More commonly, journalists will use your press release as a springboard for a larger feature story. In either case, try to develop a story as you would like to have it told. Even if your news is not reprinted verbatim, it may provide an acceptable amount of exposure.

Not everything is news. Your excitement about a certain topic does not necessarily mean that you have a newsworthy story. Think about your audience. Will someone else find your story interesting? For example, let's say you want to announce your new online business. This may be exciting news to you, but the media is used to receiving these types of releases—so what makes yours so special? Instead of just focusing on the grand opening, why not talk about the "uniqueness" of your business? What makes it so different from other online businesses? How is your online business going to make your local community a better place? Answer this question: "Why should anyone care?"—then ensure your announcement incorporates news values such as timeliness, uniqueness, or an aspect that's truly unusual. Avoid clichés such as "customers save money" or "great customer service." Focus on the elements of your news item that truly set you apart from everyone else.

Reporters and editors have to be satisfied first before they will allow you to convey your newsworthy information to the general public.

Does your press release illustrate? News outlets are looking for stories they believe have the greatest value to the majority of their listeners/viewers/readers. Give examples of how your service or product fulfills needs or satisfies desires. What benefits can be expected? Use real-life examples to powerfully communicate the benefits of using your product or service. If your company has experienced significant growth, tell the world what you did right. Show the cause and effect.

Stick to the facts. Tell the truth. Avoid fluff, embellishments, and exaggerations. If you feel your press release contains embellishments, perhaps it would be a good idea to set your press release aside until you have more exciting news to share. Journalists are naturally skeptical. If your story sounds too good to be true, you will probably hurt your own credibility. However, even if it is true, you may want to tone it down a bit.

Pick an angle. Try to make your press release timely. Tie your news to current events or social issues if possible. Make sure your story has a good news hook.

Use active, not passive, voice. Verbs in the active voice bring your press release to life. Rather than writing "entered into a partnership," use something like "is teaming up with" instead. Do not be afraid to use strong verbs as well. For example, "The committee exhibited severe hostility over the incident" reads better if changed to "The committee was enraged over the incident." Writing in this manner helps guarantee your press release will be read.

Choose your words carefully. Use only enough words to tell your story. Avoid using unnecessary adjectives, flowery language, or redundant expressions such as "added bonus" or "first time ever." If you can tell your story with fewer words, do it. Wordiness distracts from your story. Make it concise, and be sure to make each word count.

Avoid the hype. The exclamation point (!) is your enemy. There is no better way to destroy your credibility than to include a bunch of hype. If you must use an exclamation point, use one. Never do this!!!!!!!!!!!!

About your company. Your press release should end with a short paragraph that describes your company, products, and service, along with a short company history.

If you're unsure how your press release sounds after you've written it, send it to the Press Release Grader and see how it stacks up (see resource page).

If you don't feel comfortable writing your own releases though, get someone to assist you. You can either contact me or hire someone else, but ensure you or the person you hire has a good command of the English language, "cos ygwypf. Bykt," right? (See resource page to decode this message.)

Now it's time to go where the action is...

Killer Tip #5

BE WHERE THE

NEWSMAKERS ARE

"About the only thing that comes to us without effort is old age."   —*Gloria Pitzer*

There's an old saying, "If the mountain won't come to Mohammed, then Mohammed must go to the mountain." In essence, it means if journalists aren't beating down your door or blowing up your email and telephone trying to reach you, then you need to find them and take action.

This does not mean getting in your vehicle and driving all over town trying to find your local station's breaking-news van, but you can connect with journalists in a variety of proactive ways.

"The next time you want publicity you should do two things that 99 percent of other people who want publicity FAIL to do," according to Publicity Hound, Joan Stewart of publicityhound.com. The publicity expert known to millions of publicity seekers says, "First, vow that you won't use the spray and pray technique. That is, spraying the same one-size-fits-all pitch or press release to dozens or even hundreds of journalists and then praying they'll call you."

Joan adds you should also target a short list of journalists and then find out as much as you can about them before delivering your customized pitch. While doing your research you may very well discover that you have an expertise, product, or service they're interested in.

So where do you go to find the newsmakers? You can start in your own local community by checking to see if they are bloggers, and then become a subscriber. If the media outlet they work for has a website, you will more than likely be able to find links to their blogs there. Also, be sure to "like" the station's Facebook page to keep up with stories they're covering and, by all means, join in the conversation when warranted.

Look for journalists on Twitter. This is my favorite site to connect with fellow journalists. Here are just a few of the journalists you can find:

> @RebeccaJarvis
> @SamChampion
> @RobinRoberts

@ariannahuff

@TheEllenShow

@Gretawire

@AlfredEdmondJr

@PublicityHound

@katinarankin

@nprnews

@alroker

@hodakotb

@bevmahone

@donlemoncnn

One person I don't recommend you follow is Matt Lauer from NBC's *The Today Show*. He joined Twitter on December 23, 2010, and has only done three tweets—all on that one day. You definitely won't get his attention that way. Maybe he's using being a boomer as an excuse for not engaging in the Twitter community.

A couple of items I need to point out when following journalists on Twitter: Don't tell them how they can improve on their reporting skills and suggest they work harder to make you feel like Walter "the most trusted man in America" Cronkite used to. That'll get you nowhere and possibly blocked by the journalist you're trying to attract. Also, don't expect them to follow you back. Basically, they follow each other, politicians, and celebrities. And while I can't speak for them, I can say some of them do read your tweets and may respond—like Rebecca Jarvis, CBS news anchor on Saturday's edition of *The Early Show.*

While watching a segment about Thanksgiving leftovers, Rebecca and her co-host, Russ Mitchell, competed to see who could create the best post-Thanksgiving sandwich with Chef Aaron McCargo Jr. as the judge. The segment was interrupted by our local news. I wanted to know who won, so I tweeted her:

@RebeccaJarvis Who won the sandwich contest? Our local news INTERRUPTED the network :(

@BevMahone My buddy @russcbs won it by a bacon slice!

If you're not sure which reporters, producers, editors, radio talk-show hosts, and other journalists you'd like to follow, try these locations:

Muckrack.com: Muck Rack tracks thousands of journalists on Twitter and other social media. This one is my personal favorites because it's very easy to navigate, and you can see what journalists are talking about in real time.

Twellow.com: This is another one of those sites that lists journalists from everywhere, and breaks them down into subcategories.

JournalistTweets.com: The site helps journalists connect with each other. If you have a Twitter account, you can click on the gray arrow below any tweet to reply to that journalist right there.

Listorious.com: Listorious promotes itself as having the best Twitter people search on the Web, so you can find anyone by topic, region, or profession.

HelpaReporter.com: This is a site I've used both as a journalist and as a source for other journalists. Close to thirty-thousand media sources have reached out to HARO to find quotable sources and guests to interview. Sign-up is very easy, and it's the brainchild of Peter Shankman.

PitchRate.com: Promotes itself as giving free and instant access to the media. By making it easy for you to connect with journalists in need of your expertise, PitchRate helps you land the kind of media coverage that boosts your exposure and catapults you and your business to the next level.

If you use HelpaReporter.com or PitchRate.com, here's more good advice from publicity expert Joan Stewart:

Stay on topic: If you see a query from a journalist whose attention you'd love to attract, but the query isn't a good fit for your story, don't pitch off topic or the journalist might blacklist you.

Keep your pitch short: If you're responding by email, write no more than one screen of copy. Give only enough information to let the journalist know what you have to add to the story. Don't try to tell the entire story in your response.

Be patient. Don't assume that they're not interested just because they don't respond after you make a pitch. Story ideas come up for journalists all the time and then get put on the back burner for a bigger story. But believe me, if they think it's a good one, they'll hold on to it, and on a slow news day, you may get a phone call, email, or perhaps a text message, and it will be your time to shine.

In the next chapter, I'll tell you how you can get the media to come to you.

Killer Tip #6

HOST SEMINARS

AND WORKSHOPS

"You have gifts to give to the world, so find your voice and prosper."　　　*—Beverly Mahone*

Remember all those times you sat in a boring office meeting with a boss who talked on and on—and you said to yourself, "If I were in his shoes, I know I'd do a much better job"? Well, now here's your chance.

Hosting a seminar or workshop in your local community is not only a great way to promote your business, but it's another opportunity to create a buzz about you and your field of expertise.

Before you decide to host this type of event, however, you must be clear on your intent. If it's solely for the purpose of getting potential customers, this is not something the media would be interested in. They're not in the business of helping you sell your products or services. If you're offering free and valuable information that's newsworthy, you can surely grab some media attention. Journalists are always looking for experts—not salespeople—to interview.

Let's say, for example, you're a financial counselor. You could conduct a free seminar for couples who have college-bound kids or for people 50-plus. In a struggling economy, people are always looking for ways to save money, and these types of seminars would certainly be of interest to the media—provided you pitch them the correct way.

After you've decided to host a seminar, decide on a location. Community colleges are always looking for people with a certain business expertise to share their knowledge with others. Not only will they help you promote it through their media channels, but they may also offer a small stipend.

Other places to consider for your workshop:

- Local library
- High schools (career day)
- Local colleges and universities
- Churches
- Hotels

If you need time to get up your nerve to speak in front of large groups, practice by conducting a teleseminar. This is very similar to a telephone conference call. You invite prospective clients/customers to call into a specific phone number that also includes a six-digit pin code. Depending on what conference calling service you use, you can have up to one hundred people on your call at the same time. Most conferencing services are set up where you, as the moderator, have control over muting the call or not. If the call is muted, then only the moderator can speak; if the call isn't muted, then anyone can speak. You can either set up your teleseminar to have someone interview you, or do all the talking yourself.

The groovy thing about conducting teleseminars is they can last as short or as long as you like. You can have the call recorded for later use, and a transcript created for those who weren't able to dial in.

Here are a few sites to consider for hosting your teleseminar:

- Freeconferencecall.com
- Freeconference.com
- Rondee.com
- Gotomeeting.com
- Dimdim.com
- Vyew.com
- Groupme.com

It's important that the content for your teleseminar serves a purpose, such as to solve a problem or educate the listener.

Once you've got your seminars and workshops ready to go, it's up to you to create the buzz—so everyone, including the media, will know about it. That means sending a press release announcing your event, as well as posting it to places like: your website, your newsletter r ezine, your blog, your Facebook page, LinkedIn, any forums you belong to, and your local media outlets' calendar-of-events page. You should also tweet it out to those journalists you're connected with on Twitter. I would even go as far as to include it in my email signature.

Here are a few other sites where you can post your event announcements:

- Events Setter
- Events.org
- See You On The Call
- Planet Teleclass
- Seminar Announcer
- Self Growth

Now, if you've followed tips 1 through 6 and haven't created any media buzz yet, it's time to pull out the big guns...

Killer Tip #7

BE THE

MEDIA

"To succeed at gaining free publicity, you must have the imagination to generate real news that is worthy of publication or broadcast, the contacts to whom you can offer your news, and the persistence to follow through."—Jay Conrad Levinson, author of the book Guerrilla Marketing

If the media isn't coming to you, then it's up to you to find a way to reach them beyond the "follow" on Twitter, Facebook, etc.

You can do this by simply creating your own media platform. Today, with the insurgence of Internet radio, YouTube™, Blip.TV, Vimeo, social-networking sites, ezine articles, etc., you can now literally reach out to millions of people around the world.

○ ○ ○ ○ ○○○○○○○○○○○○○○○○○○ ○ ○ ○

Don't let technology stand in your way. I'll be the first to admit that I was pretty resistant to Web 2.0 and all of the other technological mumbo jumbo when I first jumped online in 2006—but just like the fear of riding a bicycle, I knew I had to overcome it if I was going to become a successful boomerpreneur.

Because there's so much out there to learn, you need to first decide the best direction for you to take to be seen AND heard. I chose blogging for two reasons: (1) I'm a writer and I enjoy it, and (2) I saw it as a way to promote my first book.

As someone who has done her share of radio and television talk shows over the past 30 years, I can tell you I struggled and was often frustrated when I first started working with BlogTalkRadio℠.

BlogTalk radio is a wonderful medium, because it's given permission to literally thousands of radio-host wannabes to create their own live talk shows. All you need is a computer and a telephone. Now, I don't want to mislead you into believing it is a very simple process because it isn't—especially if technology isn't one of your good friends. But there are tutorials on the blogtalkradio.com site, and if you research, you can find instructors who will teach you how to produce and host your own show.

Podcasting is another avenue you can explore. It is another form of audio broadcasting on the Internet.

All you need to create your own is a microphone, a computer, some software to upload your finished product, and the gift of gab.

A podcast can be made with the recording program Audacity and a hosting website. Podomatic.com is the host site I prefer.

Good, rich content is what many people are looking for and podcasting is an ideal way to showcase your expertise in a particular field. Podomatic and iTunes (see resource page) are two of a number of sites where you can upload your audio to reach the masses. I might point out that iTunes, like many other podcast hosting sites, require that you have a valid account.

If Internet radio or podcasting isn't for you, consider video marketing. Using videos is a great way to get your name out there. Unlike social networking, video marketing allows people to place a name with a face and that adds even more credibility to who you say you are. Video marketing allows you to control exactly what you want the viewer to see and it gives you an opportunity to be creative. And depending on how innovative you really are, you could wind up on one of the national morning TV talk programs. ABC's *Good Morning America* actively seeks and promotes interesting videos they find on YouTube, and viewers are invited to submit interesting things they've recorded.

CNN offers citizen journalists an opportunity to tell their stories at CNN iReport.

I recommend placing a video on your website or blog that introduces *you*. If the media is interested, having the video on your site makes it easy for them to pre-screen you to determine if you're radio or television friendly.

The media can't be everywhere all the time, and since budget cutbacks have created smaller staffs, you can help them out by submitting newsworthy material. If your local newspaper can't cover your event, send them the pictures *after* the fact. But don't send them pictures of people sitting around in a meeting—unless it's a room full of well-known, recognizable celebrities.

Certain local television stations have been known to accept video, but I recommend you call the news desk in advance to see if it's something they would be interested in. And whatever you do, don't charge them to use your video, since they will be giving you credit for it. If they choose not to use it, you can post your video on YouTube and your website, and still direct journalists there.

If you're an author, think of ways you can tie your book into a current news event. Or better yet, create your own media news event. Romance authors, for example, should always be able to capitalize during the holidays—especially Valentine's Day.

Become the expert on video by sharing your knowledge with a number of sixty-second video clips that you can post and then tweet the link to everyone in your Twitter stream or on your Facebook page. Media folks look for experts on news events all the time. For example, during the holiday season, travel is always a story. If you're a travel agent, you should have something to say about travel, as it relates to your business.

Whatever path you choose in becoming your own media, make

sure you share your video, audio and articles with as many people as possible—because you never know who knows who.

Sooner or later, you'll find out that someone in the media has gotten wind of what you're doing and wants to share your ideas and expertise with the world.

Killer Tip #8

RE-DO, RE-NEW,

RE-CREATE,

RE-INVENT!

"People who cannot invent and reinvent themselves must be content with borrowed postures, secondhand ideas, fitting in instead of standing out." —*Warren G. Bennis*

When I left my television news job in 2006, I didn't know exactly what I was going to do for the rest of my life, but I definitely knew I didn't want to go back to corporate America. I decided to market the skills I had acquired as a journalist to train others how to market themselves to the media.

Many baby boomers, like me, are quickly finding out that the "golden years of retirement," as we once described them, no longer exist. Whether we leave the workforce voluntarily or are forced out because of technology or younger employees, we now find ourselves having to create an Act II before the curtain falls for the last time.

What did I learn at the age of 49? Well, I learned that starting a business goes against everything corporate America taught me. When you work for someone else, you're instructed to go with the flow, play nicely in the sandbox, and be a team player. The game plan changes, however, as you move from the comfort and security of the corporate world into the unknown and uncertainty of being a boomerpreneur or small-business owner. All of a sudden, it is all about *you*—your rules, your sandbox and, yes, you become the "I" in team.

Becoming successful at mid-life takes time, effort, courage, and a certain drive—but it can be one of the most rewarding and best things you do at midlife.

The first step you have to take is to believe you can do anything you want to do, no matter what your age.

Did you know Laura Ingalls Wilder didn't publish her first novel until she was 65 years old? Her *Little House* series spawned 12 books and created the hit TV show *Little House on the Prairie,* which will live in the hearts and minds of the boomer generation forever.

Comedian Nipsey Russell didn't get his big break until he performed on the *Ed Sullivan Show* in his forties, and seventy-five-year-old comedienne, Moms Mabley, became the oldest person ever to have a Top-40 hit when her rendition of "Abraham, Martin and John" climbed to number 35 on the Billboard charts in the summer of 1969. If they can do it against all odds, you can too!

The next step is to design, develop, and implement your Life Reinvention Business Plan.

It's one thing to have faith and a vision, but without a plan of action, your business goals may never pan out. Before you decide to go into business for yourself, keep in mind that you need direction. That means you *need* a plan—and your plan must include creating the kind of image the media will notice.

Finally, you need to dream BIG. Every success story starts with big dreams. If you're going to be a successful entrepreneur, you have to believe the sky's the limit. Just making enough to pay the bills or getting a few customers is not enough of an aspiration to fuel you forward. Have you ever heard Oprah say all she ever wanted to do was just pay the rent and get by? No. She had big dreams.

No doubt, the journey to becoming a successful boomerpreneur in business won't be an easy one, but you can do it with determination, motivation, inspiration, and *perseverance.*

Now go forth and kill 'em with your new media savvy—because it's *Your Time to Shine!*

Killer Tip Bonus

CONTROVERSY

SELLS!

"The ultimate measure of a man is not where he stands in moments of comfort and convenience, but where he stands at times of challenge and controversy." —Martin Luther King, Jr.

Whether you like it or not, controversy sells. Journalists look for it. They thrive on it because they know it gains readers, viewers, and listeners.

Why do you think Rush Limbaugh is so popular? It's not because he's a great journalist who represents the political conservative view. Rush is extreme in his views and, often times, makes statements just to get people so riled up that he stays in the news for days, weeks and even months at a time. If that's his strategy for more media exposure, it's a good one—whether anyone likes it or not.

According to marketing expert and professional speaker George Torok, controversy helps you develop a powerful branding strategy. In George's article, *Branding Secret: Controversy Sells*, he says, "Offend someone and attract your target market. But you have to pick your position and enemies carefully. Don't offend your fans or best customers."

Torok also says, "You can also use controversy to sell your product, service or yourself. Controversy can be a powerful branding technique. But it comes with a cost. It means that you will need to take a position. You will offend some and strongly attract those who like your position. Are you willing to be so bold?"

It's that boldness that can make a journalist take notice because the controversial stand you take on something can become a very powerful promotion and may give you more publicity than you may have been seeking.

Resource Pages

Press Release Sites

Evaluate your written press release here: www.pressreleasegrader.com/

www.prlog.com

www.free-press-release.com

www.24-7pressrelease.com

www.PR.com

www.1888pressrelease.com

Places to post your teleseminars and workshops

Events Setter
http://www.eventsetter.com/

Events.org
http://www.events.org/

See You On The Call
http://seeyouonthecall.com/

Planet Teleclass
http://www.planetteleclass.com/

Seminar Announcer
http://seminarannouncer.com/

AuthorsDen
http://www.authorsden.com

Podcast Directories

iTunes—iTunes podcast directory
Requires iTunes installed to make
entry and an iTunes account.
http://www.apple.com/itunes/affiliat
es/download/

Podcast Alley
http://www.podcastalley.com/add_a_
podcast.php

All Podcasts
http://allpodcasts.com

Podfeed
http://www.podfeed.net/add_podcast.asp

Podcast Blaster
http://www.podcastblaster.com/direc
tory/add-podcast/

Blog Explosion
http://www.blogexplosion.com/mem
bers/podcast_main.php-

Digital Podcasts - podcast directory
http://www.digitalpodcast.com/

Fluctu8
http://www.fluctu8.com/add-
podcast.php

Get A Podcast
http://www.getapodcast.com/AddFee
d.aspx- podcast directory

Learn Out Loud
http://www.learnoutloud.com/Podca
st-Directory

Article Marketing

Self Growth
http://www.selfgrowth.com/

Suggested Reading

Branding Secrets: Controversy Sells
George Torok
http://www.Torok.com

50 Power Marketing Tips
George Torok
http://www.PowerMarketing.ca

Translation of language from the
NetLingo Internet Dictionary *(from Killer Tip number 4)*
http://www.netlingo.com/word/bykt.
php

"cos ygwypf. Bykt" means "Because
you get what you pay for. But you
knew that?"

Blog Directories

Technorati
http://technorati.com

Delightful Blogs
http://delightfulblogs.com

Blogorama
http://blogorama.com

Blogbunch
http://blogbunch.com

Icerocket
http://icerocket.com

Feedburner
http://feedburner.com

Bloggeries
http://bloggeries.com

Bloggernity
http://bloggernity.com

Blogged
http://blogged.com

Blogtopsites
http://blogtopsites.com

Pingomatic
http://pingomatic.com

Digg
http://digg.com

Pingoat
http://pingoat.com

Alltop
http://alltop.com

Radio Shows and Podcasts

The Boomer Beat with Beverly Mahone www.beverlymahone.com

Airs Mondays on WCOM Radio in Carrboro, NC. Looking for guests who are starting over at midlife and others who want to share their reinvention journey. This includes first-time published authors, small business owners, entrepreneurs, etc.

It's a "live" one-hour music/talk format from 12pm – 1pm EST.

Prefer live in-studio guests but will consider others who have subject matters of interest to baby boomers 919-491-0154 or email: Beverly@talk2bev.com

WCOM can be heard of 103.5fm or via live stream at www.wcomfm.org

The Boomer Beat TV Show airs in Durham, Chapel Hill and Carrboro, NC Saturdays on channel 18.

Who You Callin' Old with Dr. Cecile Forte www.mcecileforte.com

Name of Host: Dr. Cecile Forte; Theme: aging; boomers; women over 40. Where Aired: BlogTalkRadio.

Guest Profile: We look for a variety of guests who are changing the face of aging (people 40 plus). We welcome entrepreneurs, life coaches, authors, fashion experts, health and fitness experts. We have a special segment called still a chick lit, fiction and nonfiction by and for women over 40.

Email:publicrelations@cantonsmith agency.com

http://www.blogtalkradio.com/who-you-calling-old.com

Best Method of Contact: Snail mail, email:publicrelations@cantonsmith agency.com

Careers from the Kitchen Table
with Raven Blair Davis

www.careersfromthekitchentable.com

Airs live on Talk 650 Radio every Saturday at 2:00 p.m. CST, CFKT. Target: men and women (home based businesses and enthusiasts) who are looking to spend more time at home with their children, perhaps have lost their job or have been forced into early retirement and are looking for ways to create a consistent income all from the comfort of their own home.

Raven Blair-Davis
Phone: (800) 431-0842
Fax: (443) 703-7475

GirlTalk with Marlo

http://girltalkwithmarlo.com

Guests to speak about women's issues/special features about women chat@girltalkwithmarlo.com or 204-999-6680

People can listen live/on demand at http://girltalkwithmarlo.com

The Bill Marlow Show

www.billmarlowshow.com

Guest Inquiries:

comments@thebillmarlowshow.com

Bill does a 30-minute interview format on sales, management, sales management, marketing and personal achievement.

Boomer and the Babe Network
www.boomerandthebabe.com

The Boomer and The Babe Network: Giving voice to 78 million Boomers from coast to coast and border to border. Each day a different guest and a different topic. Our guests generally have a nugget or two for anyone regardless of where you might be. We hope you enjoy the relaxed conversational style of the show. Nothing fancy just Boomers sitting around the table talkin' about stuff.

www.blogtalkradio.com/boomerandbabe

ABOUT BEVERLY MAHONE

Beverly Mahone is a boomerpreneur who, after spending nearly thirty years as a radio and television journalist, is now using her media expertise to offer coaching on how to communicate effectively and market yourself and your business to newspaper, radio, and television professionals.

She is the host of a weekly radio show called The Boomer Beat on WCOM in Carrboro, NC. She also hosts a local TV show by the same name.

Beverly is also the author of three books:

(Amazon Best Seller) Whatever! A Baby Boomer's Journey Into Middle Age

Mama Said There'd Be Days Like This

Don't Ask and I Won't Have to Lie

Beverly has been classified as a baby boomer expert by the media and has appeared on numerous radio and talk programs in the United States including MSNBC-TV, FOX News, and been featured in the New York Times.

She is a contributing writer for Vibrant Nation.com and Bonkers Magazine.

Through her online marketing skills, she has created a Boomer Diva Nation, which consists of women over 50 from the U.S. and Australia.

She is also an active and popular baby boomer blogger. For more

information, you may contact her at
919-491-0154 or
beverly@talk2bev.com

http://babyboomerbev.blogspot.com
http://boomerworld.blogspot.com